Table of Conte

1. Intro

2. Grief

3. Not Me

4. Everyday is a New Beginning

5. Love Infinity

6. Finding Love Again

7. Slow and Steamy

8. Hope for the Best

9. Talk to Me

10. Guiding Light

11. Trust

12. Within the Words

Intro

Being hurt by someone you love can be a devastating experience. It can leave you feeling betrayed, angry, and afraid to trust again. However, it is possible to heal from the pain and learn to love again.

Grief

Jazz sat by the window, rain streaking down the glass mirroring the tears on her cheeks. The end had been swift, unexpected, a gut punch that left her reeling. Craig, her partner of three years, had walked out, his words a cold echo in her mind, "I'm not happy, Jazz. I've met someone else."

The first few days were a blur of disbelief, anger simmering beneath the shock. Then came the wave of grief, a tsunami of emotions she couldn't contain. She cried until her eyes burned, screamed into her pillow until her throat was raw. The pain was all-consuming, a heavy weight on her chest that made it hard to breathe.

Friends offered comfort, but their words felt hollow. How could they understand the depth of her loss? She had given Craig her heart, her trust, her dreams of a future together. And he had shattered them, leaving her to pick up the pieces.

For a while, Jazz tried to pretend she was fine, plastering on a smile, going through the motions of her daily life. But the facade was brittle, cracking under the slightest pressure. She couldn't sleep, couldn't eat, couldn't concentrate on anything. The pain was always there, a constant ache in her soul.

One night, alone in her apartment, the dam broke. She sobbed uncontrollably, the tears a release for the anger, the hurt, the betrayal. She raged against Craig, against herself, against the unfairness of it all. And then, exhausted, she curled up on the floor, allowing herself to feel the full weight of her grief.

It was in that moment of raw vulnerability that Jazz began to heal. She realized that pretending to be okay wasn't helping. She needed to grieve, to feel the pain, to let the tears flow. It was the first step towards acceptance, towards letting go, towards finding a way to love again.

Not Me

The initial shock of the breakup had faded, leaving Jazz in a state of raw vulnerability. The tears had dried, replaced by a gnawing anxiety that clung to her like a shadow. Every thought seemed to circle back to Craig, to their life together, to the bitter end.

And with those thoughts came the blame. Had she been too clingy, too demanding? Had her quirks and flaws driven him away? Maybe if she had been more understanding, more patient, more... perfect, he would still be by her side.

Her anxiety, always a low hum in the background, amplified these thoughts, turning them into a chorus of self-reproach. Sleep became a battleground, her mind replaying every perceived misstep, every imagined failing. The simplest tasks felt insurmountable, each decision a potential catastrophe.

She knew she was spiraling, but the more she tried to pull herself out, the deeper she sank. Her friends offered support, but their reassurances fell on deaf ears. After all, how could they understand the intricate workings of her mind, the relentless self-doubt that plagued her?

One day, while lost in the labyrinth of her thoughts, Jazz stumbled upon an article about dealing with heartbreak. The words seemed to jump off the screen: "Don't blame yourself." It was a simple statement, but it struck a chord deep within her.

She realized that she had been so focused on her perceived shortcomings that she had forgotten a fundamental truth: she wasn't responsible for Craig's actions. His decision to leave was his own, shaped by his own feelings and circumstances.

It was a difficult realization, one that didn't instantly erase her anxiety or self-doubt. But it was a start, a glimmer of hope in the darkness. Jazz knew that healing would take time, but she also knew that blaming herself wasn't the answer. She needed to focus on her own well-being, on rebuilding her

self-esteem, on learning to love herself

again.

Everyday is a New Beginning

The echo of the door closing behind her realtor marked a new chapter in Jazz's life. The apartment, once a shared haven, was now hers alone. It was a space filled with memories, both sweet and bitter, of a love lost.

As she arranged her belongings, each item seemed to carry a piece of the past. The laughter-filled evenings on the couch, the quiet breakfasts in the nook, the heated arguments that had once seemed insurmountable. It was a bittersweet symphony, a reminder of what was and what could have been.

In the quiet solitude of her new home, Jazz found herself reflecting on the relationship. The rose-tinted glasses of grief had faded, allowing for a clearer perspective. She saw the red flags she had ignored, the compromises she had made, the patterns of behavior that, in hindsight, were clear indicators of incompatibility.

It was a painful realization, but also a necessary one. Jazz understood that to move forward, she needed to learn from the past. She needed to identify the mistakes she had made, not to dwell on them, but to ensure she didn't repeat them.

She had loved Craig deeply, but perhaps she had loved him more than she had loved herself. She had allowed her needs and desires to be overshadowed, her voice to be silenced. She had stayed even when her intuition screamed for her to leave.

These were hard truths to confront, but Jazz faced them with a newfound determination. She vowed to never again ignore her own needs, to never again compromise her self-worth for the sake of love. She would choose her partners wisely, communicate openly and honestly, and most importantly, she would listen to her gut.

The road ahead was uncertain, but Jazz was no longer afraid. She had learned from the experience, grown stronger from the pain. She was ready to embrace her independence, to rediscover herself, to open her heart to

the possibility of a love that was healthy,

fulfilling, and true.

Love Infinity

The months following her breakup were a whirlwind of activity for Jazz. She poured herself into her work, taking on extra projects and responsibilities. She reconnected with her family, spending weekends with her parents and siblings, laughing over old stories and creating new memories. She volunteered at the local community center, tutoring children and organizing food drives.

Amidst the busyness, Jazz found solace in solitude. She deepened her prayer life, spending hours in quiet contemplation, seeking guidance and strength from her faith. She rediscovered her love of reading, devouring books on spirituality, philosophy, and personal growth. She attended workshops and retreats, connecting with like-minded individuals and exploring different paths to enlightenment.

Through this journey of self-discovery, Jazz came to a profound realization: she didn't need to shut herself off from love. The pain from her past relationship had been a powerful teacher, but it didn't define her future. She opened her heart cautiously, not rushing into anything new, but allowing herself to see the possibilities.

She met Ben at a community event, a kind and compassionate man with a gentle smile and a shared passion for service. Their friendship blossomed slowly, built on mutual respect, shared values, and a deep sense of connection. Jazz found herself drawn to Ben's warmth and sincerity, his ability to listen without judgment, an his unwavering support for her dreams and aspirations.

It wasn't always easy. There were moments of doubt, flashes of fear, echoes of past hurts. But Jazz had learned to trust her instincts, to communicate her needs openly and honestly, to embrace vulnerability without losing sight of her self-worth.

With Ben, Jazz experienced a love that was different from anything she had known before. It was a love that was patient and kind, that celebrated her strengths and accepted her flaws, that encouraged her growth and supported her independence. It was a love that didn't complete her, but complemented her, enriching her life in countless ways.

Jazz had learned that love, like life, was a journey, not a destination. There would be challenges along the way, but she was no longer afraid to face them. She had learned from her past, grown stronger from her pain, and opened her heart to the possibility of a love that was healthy, fulfilling, and true.

Finding Love Again

In depths of pain, where shadows dwell,

Love's flame flickers, fragile, frail.

Hearts once broken, spirits scarred,

By wounds inflicted, guarded hard.

Yet, a whisper soft, a gentle plea,

Reminds us of a love so free.

A love divine, a love so pure,

Unfailing, steadfast, ever sure.

Though we have strayed, His grace remains,

Forgiving faults, easing pains.

His love endures, a beacon bright,

Guiding us through the darkest night.

So, let us not, in fear retreat,

But seek His wisdom, love to meet.

With open hearts, and spirits brave,

We'll find the love our souls crave.

For in His love, we find our worth,

And learn to love, like Him, on earth.

With faith as our guide, and hope as our

light,

We'll love again, with all our might.

Slow and Steamy

The first date with Ben was everything Jazz had hoped for and more. The movie was enjoyable, the dinner delicious, and the conversation flowed effortlessly. They laughed, they shared stories, they discovered common interests and unexpected connections.

As the evening drew to a close, Ben invited Jazz back to his place for a glass of wine. His apartment was warm and inviting, filled with books, music, and personal touches that spoke of a life well-lived. Jazz felt comfortable and at ease in his presence, the lingering pain of her past fading into the background.

They settled on the sofa, wine glasses in hand, and talked for hours. The conversation meandered from lighthearted banter to deeper topics, each revelation drawing them closer. Jazz was captivated by Ben's intelligence, his wit, his genuine interest in her thoughts and feelings.

As the night wore on, the atmosphere grew increasingly intimate. The soft glow of the lamp, the crackling fire, the gentle brush of Ben's hand against hers... it all conspired to create a moment of undeniable attraction.

Jazz felt a familiar pull, a desire to surrender to the moment, to let the passion take over. But then, a voice of reason whispered in her ear: "Take things slow."

She remembered the lessons she had learned, the importance of building a solid foundation before diving headfirst into a relationship. She didn't want to repeat the mistakes of her past, to rush into something that might not be right for her in the long run.

With a gentle smile, Jazz excused herself to the restroom, giving herself a moment to gather her thoughts. She splashed water on her face, took a deep breath, and reminded herself that this was just the first date. There was no need to rush, no pressure to take things further than she was comfortable with.

When she returned to the living room, Ben was waiting for her, his expression patient and understanding. Jazz felt a surge of gratitude for his respect, his willingness to let her set the pace.

They finished their wine, talked a little longer, and then Ben walked her to her car. As they said goodnight, Jazz felt a sense of peace and contentment. She had enjoyed the evening immensely, but she was also proud of herself for listening to her inner voice and taking things slow.

The road ahead was still uncertain, but Jazz was no longer afraid. She had learned from her past, grown stronger

from her pain, and opened her heart to

the possibility of a love that was built on

trust, respect, and a genuine

connection.

Hope for the Best

As Jazz and Ben's relationship deepened, they began to share more intimate details about their lives. One evening, over a candlelit dinner, Ben opened up about his family. His parents were getting older, and living several states away weighed heavily on his heart. He tried to visit them as often as possible, but the distance and the demands of his job made it a challenge.

Jazz listened attentively, a knot forming in her stomach. Ben's words painted a picture of a devoted son, a responsible and caring man. Yet, a nagging doubt crept into her mind. Her past experiences had taught her to be wary, to question the motives of those who seemed too good to be true.

She remembered the countless times her ex had used work commitments or family obligations as an excuse to hide his indiscretions. The late nights, the unanswered calls, the vague explanations that always left her feeling uneasy and insecure.

A wave of anxiety washed over Jazz. Was Ben truly the kind and trustworthy man he appeared to be, or was he just another player in disguise? Should she trust her instincts and the nagging feeling that something wasn't quite right?

As she wrestled with these thoughts, Jazz reminded herself of the lessons she had learned. She had vowed to listen to her gut, to be cautious and discerning when it came to matters of the heart. But she had also promised herself that she wouldn't let her past experiences define her future.

Jazz took a deep breath and looked Ben in the eyes. "I appreciate you sharing this with me," she said, her voice steady. "It sounds like your family means a lot to you."

Ben smiled, his gaze warm and sincere. "They do," he replied. "And I hope you'll get to meet them someday."

Jazz nodded, a flicker of hope igniting within her. Perhaps Ben was different.

Perhaps he was the kind of man who could be trusted, who would honor her feelings and respect her boundaries.

She decided to keep her heart open, but her eyes wide open as well. She would continue to get to know Ben, to observe his actions, to listen to her intuition. If something felt off, she wouldn't hesitate to walk away. But for now, she would give him the benefit of the doubt, and allow herself to hope for the best.

Talk to Me

In the garden of love, where two hearts

entwine,

Communication blooms, a bond so

divine.

Speak your truth, with courage and

grace,

Let honesty flow, in every embrace.

Share your fears, your dreams, your

deepest desires,

With words that ignite, like passionate

fires.

Listen closely, with an open heart,

To the whispers of love, from the very start.

When shadows of doubt, or storms cloud the sky,
Communicate freely, don't let feelings lie.
With honesty as your guiding light,
Love's path will be clear, shining ever so bright.

In the dance of connection, let words be the song,
Open and honest, where you both belong.

For in the game of love, so beautifully spun,

Communication is key, till the setting of the sun.

Guiding Light

Several months into her budding relationship with Ben, Jazz found herself navigating a delicate balance between hope and caution. The wounds from her past were still tender, a constant reminder of the fragility of trust and the potential for heartbreak. Yet, she refused to let those experiences dictate her future.

Ben had proven to be a kind, compassionate, and patient partner. He respected her boundaries, communicated openly and honestly, and never pressured her to move faster than she was comfortable with. Jazz appreciated his understanding, his willingness to let the relationship unfold naturally.

Still, she couldn't shake the feeling that she needed to keep her options open. She wasn't ready to fully commit to Ben, to close herself off to other possibilities. She wanted to explore, to experience, to ensure that he was truly the right person for her.

So, Jazz continued to date casually, meeting new people, going on occasional outings, and keeping her heart open to potential connections. She didn't hide this from Ben, explaining that she was still healing, still learning to trust again.

Ben accepted her decision with grace, assuring her that he was willing to wait, to give her the time and space she needed. He understood that trust was earned, not given, and he was committed to proving himself worthy of her love.

Jazz was grateful for his patience, his unwavering support. She knew that finding the perfect person wasn't going to happen overnight. It was a journey, a process of discovery and growth. And she was willing to be patient, to keep looking, to trust that the right person was out there for her.

In the meantime, she would continue to enjoy her time with Ben, to nurture their growing connection, to see where the path might lead. And she would remain open to other possibilities, knowing that ultimately, her heart would guide her to

the love she deserved.

Trust

In the bustling city of Atlanta, amidst the towering skyscrapers and the ceaseless hum of traffic, lived a woman named Jae. Jae had always been a trusting soul, wearing her heart on her sleeve and seeing the good in everyone. However, a painful betrayal from a past relationship had shattered her trust, leaving her guarded and hesitant to open her heart again.

For years, Jae had built emotional walls, shielding herself from potential hurt. She avoided deep connections, keeping her relationships superficial and fleeting. The fear of being vulnerable, of being hurt again, was a constant companion.

One day, Jae met John, a kind and patient man with a warm smile on a dating app. John was different from anyone she had ever met. He was attentive, understanding, and genuinely interested in getting to know her. Slowly, Jae began to let her guard down, sharing her thoughts, her dreams, and her fears with him.

John's unwavering support and consistent actions helped Jae rebuild her trust. He was always there for her, through thick and thin, proving his reliability and commitment. With time, Jae realized that not everyone was like her ex. She learned that vulnerability could be a strength, not a weakness, and that opening her heart could lead to incredible joy.

As Jae and John's relationship blossomed, she discovered the beauty of trust. She learned to let go of her past hurts, to embrace the present, and to look forward to a future filled with love

and happiness. Jae had found love

again, and with it, the courage to trust.

Within the Words

The dim glow of the bar cast long shadows across the polished wood of the table where Jae and John sat, drinks in hand. The clinking of ice in their glasses punctuated the comfortable silence that had fallen between them. They had spent the evening laughing, sharing stories, and delving into the depths of each other's personalities through playful questions and witty banter.

Jae, her cheeks flushed from a combination of the alcohol and the warmth of John's company, found herself drawn to his easy smile and genuine laughter. She had been hesitant to agree to this date, her past experiences casting a long shadow of doubt over her ability to trust again. But John, with his patient nature and sincere interest, had slowly chipped away at her defenses, revealing the vulnerable heart that beat beneath her guarded exterior.

As the night wore on, their conversation turned to deeper topics, their shared dreams and aspirations, their fears and vulnerabilities. Jae found herself opening up to John in a way she hadn't done in years, sharing her past hurts and her hopes for the future.

John listened intently, his eyes never leaving hers, his expression a mixture of empathy and admiration. When she finished speaking, he reached across the table, his hand hovering hesitantly above hers. "Jae," he said, his voice soft and sincere, "I know you've been hurt in the past, and I would never do anything to break your trust. But I'm enjoying this evening so much, and I'm wondering if I could be so bold as to ask if I could touch your leg?"

Jae's heart skipped a beat. The simple request, so respectful and considerate, spoke volumes about John's character. She looked into his eyes, searching for any hint of insincerity, but found only warmth and genuine affection.

A shy smile spread across her face as she nodded, her heart fluttering with a mix of nervousness and excitement. John's hand, warm and gentle, came to rest on her leg, sending a shiver of anticipation through her body.

As they sat there, their hands intertwined, their eyes locked in a silent promise of trust and connection, Jae knew that she had taken a chance on love again. And for the first time in a long time, she felt a glimmer of hope for the future.

Made in the USA
Columbia, SC
12 November 2024